In The Hands of Jesus

Barbara Morris

Barbara Morris

ISBN: 978-1-7320181-2-9

All scripture quotation is taken from the NIV translation unless otherwise stated.

Holy Bible, New International Version®, NIV® Copyright ©1973, 1978, 1984, 2011 by Biblica, Inc.® Used by permission. All rights reserved worldwide.

Cover designed by Latoya Anderson
Llaenterprizes@gmail.com

Published by: A.T. Destiny Awaits Group LLC
atdestinyawaits.com

I GIFT THIS BOOK TO

_____

THIS _____ DAY OF

_____, _____.

WITH LOVE,

_____

AMEN.

Barbara Morris

DEDICATION

I dedicate this book to my daughter Leandra Brandon. She has been my encourager, inspiration and has brought me much joy.

Although, she wasn't born at the time of my miracle, I shared it with her when she got older. She always gave praise to God for what he had done in her mother's life. She was raised in the Church and has since experienced a miracle of her own. Although she was told she couldn't have children, I'm blessed to be a grandmother.

Thank you, Leandra, for celebrating with me, what only God has done.

Barbara Morris

TABLE OF CONTENTS

ACKNOWLEDGMENTS

First, Lord, Thank You for allowing this book to have been a part of your plans for me. Lord, I thank You. My life represents that it was only you, Lord. You are the only one that will forever get the Glory for allowing me to live to see my children grown and experience becoming a grandmother, Thank you, Jesus.

Now, I would like to take the time by using this space to acknowledge those of you that has pushed me to success with the help of the Lord.

A Special Thank you to my Pastor Jevon Goode of Destiny Church in Dothan, Alabama. I'm grateful that you preached so strong on picking your dream up again. I heard it, received it and I'm doing it. Thank you so much for seeing in me what was lying dormant. It came to life.

To my close friends, you all know who you are. Thank you for always having a listening ear and constantly telling me I can do this.

My Testimony
GOD, MY MIRACLE WORKER

I declare God is my miracle worker. When, I was 26 years old I developed what I thought was a common cold. I had a very sore throat and was running a high temperature, but I was alert. I went to the doctor. He looked at me very funny. I remember Dr. Smeradi saying to me, "We got to get you to the hospital now. You are a very sick girl." I then, fearfully asked myself, "What is happening to me?"

Well, I was admitted into the hospital a week after Christmas. Although I hated to leave my children, I knew they would be in good hands with my mom.

At this time, I was saved and had a personal relationship with the Lord. Now, I wasn't perfect, but I was learning the importance of having a prayer life. I wanted to be close to Jesus. I remember thinking, If I never needed the Lord, I sure do need him now.

When I got to the Stamford Connecticut hospital, they began to run all kind of test. My condition became worse. I was connected to every machine you could think of, such as a heart machine, ice bed machine which was like a long rubber mat along with others. This was to help with controlling my body temperature.

I remember experiencing swelling all over my body like I was pregnant. Props were placed in my bed to keep the sheet from touching my body.

Although, I had a total of 18 doctors working on my individual case, they didn't have any answers even after me being there for three weeks. My condition continued to worsen. They kept me isolated. No one was allowed to enter without total head to toe coverage. I was isolated for a total of eight weeks.

One morning, in particular, I can remember being swollen and fever was cooking my body. I looked over to the back of the room in the corner and there stood a man dressed in all black, in a hat and suit even his shoes were all black. He stood there staring right at me.

Now, my God Father Elder Tate arrived as usual to pray and check on me. I couldn't speak because my tongue was swollen when I noticed the man standing there, I began to pray. My God Father was a man of God and when he saw what I saw, he began to rebuke death and began speaking life in my room. He came close to me, looked at the frame of man standing in the corner and said to him, you can't have her. She belongs to God. He continued to speak to the evil presence stating, "Get out of here, the Blood of Jesus is against you! Go Now!"

Then the unimaginable happened, I actually saw this man in black glide across the room to my bed, look at me and then he glided right out of my room.

Praise God for being my miracle worker!

At that time in my life, I was a person that would pray when things were going well not just when things weren't well. The word of God tells us to pray always and not cease from praying. Thank God I remembered his word in my time of need.

I received life and not death. A week passed and I began to get better, but yet that's not the end. It was on the weekend. During this time my fever grew worse. The nurse called my doctor.

He came in the room and I saw about three nurses with him.

I remember Dr. Smeradi speaking to me and saying, "Ms. Barbara, if you began to hear bells ringing let us know. We will need to wheel you to ICU."

Then all of them just stared at my bed looking, waiting, anticipating, ready, and willing to do what the doctor said. One nurse asked, "Do you hear anything?" She squeezed my hand. I could hear her, but I was in the presence of the Lord. I was singing and worshiping Jesus.

I remember this happened on the weekend because that Sunday afternoon Prophet Bobby Davis at Miracle Faith Temple was preaching the word. I was later told that he stopped in the service and called my name very plain and clear and exclaiming that I shall live and not die.

I believe at that very moment the

fever began to break. Big drops of sweat hit my back. I began to make a moaning sound. The nurse came over to my bed and saw I was soaked in sweat.

They called for the doctor, he came in smiling saying truly the man upstairs loves you.

My healing was a process. It didn't all happen overnight, but as every day passed by, I was feeling and looking better.

Now let me share with you that I had lost a lot of weight, the color of my skin was much darker, my hair had fallen out, and my flesh was falling off in the bed. I remember the machines, the props, and the ice bed when it wasn't working properly. There wasn't any talk about me leaving the hospital until I was able to eat food, drink water and juices. I remember, being flat on my back for eight weeks. It damaged my balance to stand and walk. I had to relearn to walk, and the doctor felt that I would not be able to remember my family members because, at times, my fever was extremely high. Praise God, the doctor was wrong. I knew everyone and never lost my knowledge of anyone.

There were times during this process that I was not able to pray for myself because I was very sick and on the verge of dying. I believe the prayers that I had prayed in the past were built up prayers. I had no choice but rest in the arms of God. I kept hearing in my spirit, "The timber was built, it's ok, I have you." I believe God was assuring me that all the times I had prayed before entering this season of my life were working for me in my time of need.

The final explanation that all these doctors came up with was I had developed a viral disease. Which had plagued my body.

I don't know what happened, but I will forever be grateful for being alive to share my testimony with those that may need to know that Jesus is real.

God is a Good God. The Lord worked a miracle then and He still works miracles today.

I am convinced that I was in His Hands All the Time.

To   God   be   The   Glory!

Barbara Morris

PERSONAL PRAYERS

PRAYER WORKS

I take this time to encourage you to pray while you have a chance. Pray when the sun is shining and pray when it is raining in your life. You just don't know there may be days when you won't be able to say a word.

God is a faithful God, and we should strive to be faithful, also.

I hope you find the next five prayers helpful and useful in your time of need.

Prayer is a mandate from God, and it works.

PRAYER WORKS

IN MY DESPERATION

Lord Jesus, You are a Great God, a loving and caring God. Your word says that You are a present help in the time of trouble. I need You, Jesus, to breathe life into me now. Jesus, I'm trying to hold on until your healing manifests. I need you to help me because fear is trying to creep in on me. My children need me, God, please help. I must live and not die. Lord the pain, and fever are too much for me. I ask You in the name of Jesus to bring life to my body and mind. Thank You in Jesus name, I pray. And it is so,

Amen

WHEN I NEEDED A MOMENT OF COMFORT

Father God, in the name of Jesus, I come to you Father thanking you for your word. I need you to touch me. I believe but help my unbelief. You promise in your word that you will never leave me, you said you will always be here. Lord, I need your healing hands, right now, Lord, to touch my feeble body.

Thank you, Jesus, for your word that decrees and declares that you are a present help in the time of trouble. You are the God that will keep his promises. I am the healed of the Lord, Your words says so, I believe, and now I receive my healing manifestation.

Thank you for your word because there is power, life, and strength in it. I do receive in Jesus name.   *Amen*

IN MY MOMENT OF UNCERTAINTY-DOUBT

Lord, Jesus, here I am, Lord, fighting the doubt that is coming against my mind. You have always been there for me in the past. I have no choice but to believe in you. You have been there for me from the beginning until now. You have healed me. I will not give up. I will press because I trust you. I am your child, so I know that you want me to live a more abundant life and not die. You are the same God that did it before, and I ask that you do it again. Thank you, Jesus, for loving me. Your healing virtue is flowing through me, and I still believe in Jesus name.

Amen

AT THE POINT OF VICTORY

Father, I will be forever grateful for all that you have done. It was you that put my flesh back in order. You caused me to remain in my right frame of mind.

Lord, I am the head and not the tail because of you. I am above and not beneath. I believe the report of the Lord that says I am healed. The pains in my body will go away. My fever will come down and leave my body alone. I belong to the Most High God. You are my Father. My body will operate as you created it to do. Thank you, Lord, I will speak what You say about me, and it shall manifest. I praise your name

Amen

MY PRAYER FOR YOU

Lord, I pray for everyone reading this book. Father, I pray that they will receive your mental, spiritual, and healing manifestation in the name of Jesus.

Father, You are the Lord of lords and the King of kings. Father touch each of them. Encourage them through your Holy word. Encourage them to know that they are worth fighting for.

Lord, thank you for loving each of them so much.

Father teach them how to say what you say about them. Lord, draw them close to you. Father teach them the importance of worship, prayer, and spending time in your word. Lord, fill them deep in their hearts that it can't be stolen from them. Thank you, Lord, God in Jesus name,

Amen

Barbara Morris

Favorite Biblical Promises

Jeremiah 29:11

For I know the plans I have for you," declares the Lord, "plans to prosper you and not to harm you, plans to give you hope and a future.

Psalm 91:10-11

no harm will overtake you, no disaster will come near your tent. For he will command his angels concerning you to guard you in all your ways;

Isaiah 26:3
You will keep in perfect
peace
those whose minds are
steadfast,
because they trust in you.

Deuteronomy 3:6
We completely destroyed[a]
them, as we had done with
Sihon king of Heshbon,
destroying[b] every city—
men, women and children.

Isaiah 43:2

When you pass through the
waters,
I will be with you;
and when you pass through
the rivers,
they will not sweep over
you.
When you walk through the
fire,
you will not be burned;
the flames will not set you
ablaze.

Isaiah 53:5
*But he was pierced for our
transgressions,
he was crushed for our
iniquities;
the punishment that brought
us peace was on him,
and by his wounds we are
healed.*

Psalm 121

*I lift up my eyes to the
mountains—
where does my help come
from?*
*2 My help comes from the
Lord,
the Maker of heaven and
earth.*
*3 He will not let your foot
slip—
he who watches over you
will not slumber;*
*4 indeed, he who watches
over Israel
will neither slumber nor
sleep.*
*5 The Lord watches over
you—
the Lord is your shade at
your right hand;*

⁶ *the sun will not harm you*
by day,
nor the moon by night.
⁷ *The Lord will keep you from*
all harm—
he will watch over your
life;
⁸ *the Lord will watch over*
your coming and going
both now and
forevermore.

Isaiah 54:17
no weapon forged against
you will prevail,
and you will refute every
tongue that accuses you.
This is the heritage of the
servants of the Lord,
and this is their
vindication from me,"
declares the Lord.

Letter to the Reader

First and Foremost, thank you. I pray that everyone that reads this book will receive healing whether it be mental, spiritual, or physical. I pray that you receive it.

May the same Lord of Lords and King of Kings that healed my body, touch you and cause healing to manifest. Be encouraged and know you are worth fighting for and our Heavenly Father loves you so much.

It is important to say what God says about you, especially in the hard times. Draw close to God and He will draw close to you.

Take the time to worship, pray, and read his word. Get it deep within your heart and don't let nothing nor anyone can pluck it out.

May God bless you really Good,
            Elder Barbara Morris

ABOUT THE AUTHOR

Barbara Ree Morris is a mother of three, two sons and a daughter. She is a true woman that loves the Lord. She received Christ in her life at an early age. Barbara Ree Morris is a proud grandmother of a beautiful baby girl, Madison Grace Brandon. Barbara Ree Morris truly gives God all the praise and glory for all her accomplishments.

She graduated from Capps College in 2005 as a medical assistant. She later attended Destiny Bible College in Dothan, receiving a bachelor's degree in Biblical Studies in 2017. Barbara Ree Morris is a member of Destiny Church Dothan, Al. under the leadership of Dr. & Pastor Jevon Goode.